Publish Your Chapbook!

Six Weeks to Professional Publication

Amber Lea Starfire

MoonSkye Publishing

NAPA, CA

Publish Your Chapbook! — Six Weeks to Professional Publication / Amber Lea Starfire —1st Ed.

ISBN 10: 0984863664
ISBN 13: 978-0-9848636-6-2

MoonSkye Publishing
1351 2nd St. #5562
Napa CA 94581
www.moonskyepublishing.com

Contents

Introduction

A (very) Brief History of Chapbooks

The term *Chapbook* originates with 17th century peddlers, called chapmen, who traveled from town to town selling their wares. Among the wares they sold were small, pocket-sized booklets of popular literature, fairy tales, short stories, political statements, and news — often illustrated with crude woodcuts — for just a few pennies. These "chapbooks," as they came to be known, were inexpensive to produce and were typically made from one piece of paper, which was folded into four, eight, or sixteen pages and bound by stitches.

Chapbooks all but disappeared during the Industrial Revolution due to competition from cheap newspapers and from laws restricting peddling. They reappeared, however, during the 1950s when Beatniks began using the chapbook form as a way to distribute their poetry. Since then, chapbooks have become accepted as an affordable way for writers to publish their work.

While the term *chapbook* conjures up slim volumes of poetry, these days chapbooks may also contain prose and artwork, are typically from twenty to forty pages in length, and are constructed with bindings that vary from photocopied and stapled booklets to perfect-bound spines.

Why Publish Your Chapbook?

A chapbook is an excellent way to publish your work, establish your author platform, gain readers, and learn the self-publishing process. If you've felt mystified or overwhelmed by the amount of conflicting self-publishing information available, you are not alone! One could make a career out of reading and sorting out the various opinions and avenues for publishing.

That's why I'm going to show you how to publish a chapbook using CreateSpace. In doing so, the publishing process will be demystified and you'll walk away with a lovely book of poetry and/or prose to share with your readers.

Publish Your Chapbook! offers a simplified version of the entire paperback publishing process from start to finish. (In fact, this book was created using all the instructions contained within it.) I do not touch on how to create an e-book, but provide resources at the end of the book to help you convert and publish your chapbook as an e-book.

Why CreateSpace?

- It's free — there are no upfront costs to you. CreateSpace makes its money by keeping a percentage of the books you sell.

- It's easy — the site walks you through the process. I will help you further by explaining each step along the way.

- It's full of resources — CreateSpace contains a wealth of information to help you make publishing decisions.

- It's Amazon — If you choose, your chapbook will automatically be published and available on Amazon, as well as a number of other distribution avenues.

- Printing is On Demand (POD) and inexpensive.

Limitations of CreateSpace

The only real limitation I have experienced with CreateSpace is that you won't have access to distribution in bookstores, even though CreateSpace offers bookstore distribution. That's because bookstores demand a 55% discount, which CreateSpace doesn't offer. Since bookstores don't normally sell chapbooks except on consignment, this should not be an issue for you.

How to Use this Book

Publish Your Chapbook! is a step-by-step manual and workbook to assist you with publishing a small collection of writing. To get the most out of it, start at Week 1 and move methodically through each step. Check off each task as you complete it. Write notes in the margins and in the space provided for some of the tasks.

Journaling Through the Publishing Process

Over the course of the next six weeks, you'll be amazed at how much you learn and accomplish.

For this reason, I have included space at the end of each chapter for you to record your progress and thoughts about what you're learning, along with a few writing prompts to help you reflect upon the process.

Week 1: Collecting Your Work

The first steps to publishing your chapbook are to select and compile the pieces to include in your chapbook, open a CreateSpace account, and prepare your title information. This week, you'll look at what to consider when selecting your pieces, as well as how to prepare your title information.

Things to consider

Before actually compiling your chapbook, answer the following questions:

1. Why do you want to publish your chapbook?

2. Who is your ideal reader? Describe him or her.

3. What unites the pieces? Is there a theme? For example: childhood stories, family history, nature, colors, place, or humor.

4. Coherence and structure — do the pieces add up to a larger story or do they stand alone? Are they in chronological order or associative? How does one piece move to the next?

5. Number of pieces and size of your book — chapbooks are typically between 20-40 pages, including front and back matter (title and copyright pages, acknowledgements, author bio, and so on). So if you are publishing short poems, one per page, you will need between 20-35 pieces. If you are including prose, the number of pieces will depend upon the size and formatting of your finished book. I recommend a maximum of 25, 8.5 x 11-inch pages of double-spaced text.

How many pieces do you want to include?

Collecting Your Pieces in One Document

After you've selected pieces for inclusion in your chapbook, copy and paste them all into one Word document in the order in which you want them. If you're not sure about the order, paste them in any order that seems logical; you can always change the order of your pieces prior to publishing.

At this point, do not format titles, headings, or text. You will be formatting your manuscript during Weeks 2 and 3.

Opening a CreateSpace Account

If you have not already done so, go online to CreateSpace.com and create a new account by clicking the "Sign Up" button on the left side of the page. Then follow directions to complete the minimum required for a new account.

Preparing Title Information

1. Write the title of your chapbook and, if you have one, the subtitle.

2. Write the size you want your book to be and whether you want it on white or creme paper. I recommend choosing one of the following typical sizes: 5 x 8 inches, 5.25 x 8 inches, or 5.5 x 8 inches

3. When you have them, record your ISBN numbers.

   ISBN 10:

   ISBN 13:.

   "ISBN" is the acronym for International Standard Book Number. ISBNs are unique ten- or thirteen-digit numbers assigned to every published book. An ISBN identifies a title's binding, edition, and publisher, and every book must have one.

   When you publish through CreateSpace, you have three main options:
   - o   You can let CreateSpace assign an ISBN;
   - o   You can pay $10 for your own ISBN;
   - o   You can purchases ISBN numbers through Bowker.

To help you understand how ISBNs work and to decide which way is best for you, log into your CreateSpace account and read this helpful article About ISBNs: (https://www.createspace.com/Help/Index.jsp?orgId=00D300000001Sh9&id=50170000000I1ec)

4. Next, write a description of your chapbook. This is a short (under 150-word) summary of what the book is about. Write the description with your audience in mind: what will appeal to and intrigue your ideal reader?

5. Write your author bio. In your 100-word bio, you want to list your professional credentials as a writer, published works, and something personal about yourself. If you need ideas, browse Amazon and read other authors' bios.

6. Finally, pat yourself on the back for a good week's work and celebrate by doing something self-nurturing, such as going for a walk in nature or taking a long, hot bath.

Reflection

After completing the steps in this chapter, take a moment to reflect on your week's work.

- What did you learn?

- Did you run into any challenges or roadblocks? If so, what were they and how did you handle them?

- What are your thoughts about this stage of the publishing process?

Week 2: Preparing Your Manuscript

Preparing your manuscript for publication requires learning about the technology involved in publishing and, particularly, how to use the editing and formatting features in Microsoft Word. If you have not yet learned these skills, the knowledge gained by going through the copyediting and formatting steps in this and the following chapters, will help you throughout the rest of your professional writing and publishing career.

This week, we'll begin the process of copyediting and formatting your chapbook for publication. The important and extensive process of editing is too large a subject for this tutorial. However, I do present common errors and offer instructions to remedy them.

A Few Words on Copyediting

You have gone over every piece in your manuscript with care, yet errors remain. How do you find these errors, and what can you do about them? Copyediting requires attention to detail and the willingness to read your work very closely. The following steps will help you find and correct some of the most common errors.

1. **Check your spelling and grammar** using Word's Spelling Checker. If you don't know how to run the spelling checker, you can find directions by searching for "check spelling" under your Help menu.

    Be sure to double-check every entry flagged by Word. Microsoft Word isn't perfect; sometimes it flags words as wrong that are correct, and sometimes it highlights incorrect grammar that you want to remain the way it is. Each instance should be a conscious and rational choice.

2. **Check for tense agreement.** You don't want to unintentionally mix tenses within a piece. Be sure that if your piece starts out in present tense, it stays in present tense, unless in dialogue or your piece has a change of Point of View (POV). The same is

true of poetry — unless mixing the tenses is part of the poet's voice. Again, the point is to be intentional about the choices you make.

3. **Check for subject-verb agreement.** Problems with subject-verb agreement may occur when two or more subjects are joined by *and*. And be careful when using *either, neither,* and *each*; in these cases, the verb should be singular.

   Examples:

   > **Her background and experience gives** her an edge on the competition. **Change to: Her background and experience give** her an edge on the competition.

   > **My father and my mother is** focused on saving enough for retirement. **Change to: My father and my mother are** focused on saving enough for retirement.

   > **Does** rejection and acceptance affect your feelings about writing? **Change to: Do** rejection and acceptance affect your feelings about writing?

   > **Each of the men and women were** wearing their best outfits. **Change to: Each of the men and women was** wearing his or her best outfit. (With the use of each, the correct verb is singular (was), their must be changed to his or her, and outfit must also be singular. Better yet, get rid of the word *each* and change your sentence structure from a passive to an active voice: The men and women wore their best outfits.)

   > **Neither the sun nor the moon shine** on that dark corner of the garden. **Neither the sun nor the moon shines** on that dark corner of the garden. (Neither shines, not neither shine.)

4. **Check for correct use of apostrophes.** Guidelines on the use of apostrophes are more fixed than for some of the other punctuation topics, and consistent misuse of apostrophes marks your writing as amateurish, therefore it's important to have a good understanding of how and when to use them.

- Use apostrophes to show possession:

  o If a singular noun doesn't end in s, then add *'s* to show possession: the *cat's* fur, the *man's* beard, the *boy's* shirt, the *apple's* color.

  o Do not use apostrophes with possessive pronouns: *mine, yours, his, hers, its, ours, theirs.*

  o If a plural noun ends in s, place the apostrophe at the end of the word, after the s: the *cats'* whiskers, the *girls'* conversations.

  o If a plural noun does not end in s, add *'s* to the end of the word: *women's* rights, *children's* playground, *men's* coats.

  o If a singular word or name ends in s, add *'s* to the end of the word: the *Jones's* house; the *atlas's* cover. Ancient names are exceptions to this rule; add the apostrophe at the end of the name: *Jesus'* robe, *Moses'* staff, *Zeus'* lightning bolt.

- Use apostrophes to show time or quantity:

  o One *year's* work, two *dollars'* worth, five *months'* old.

- Use apostrophes for contractions and to indicate that letters are missing (usually in dialog):

  o "He'p me up. I s'pose I'm gettin' old."

  o Use *it's* for it is (not for possession).

  o Other common contractions: *there's* for there is, *here's* for here is, *you're* for you are (not your), *can't* for cannot.

- Use apostrophes to show letters as plural:

  o Two S's, five F's and seven G's.

  o Don't use apostrophes for decades: 1970s.

  o In the past, it was customary to place an apostrophe before a shortened decade: '60s, '70s, '80s, etc. However, that custom is changing and currently either '70s or 70s is acceptable.

5. **Finally — and do not skip this step! — print out your manuscript and read it to yourself out loud.** If you're not in the habit of doing this, you'll be surprised by how many mistakes or awkward phrases you uncover by reading your work aloud.

Using CreateSpace Book Templates

CreateSpace assists you with formatting your book layout by providing book templates. The templates include document size, mirrored margins adequate for the book, and page headers and footers.

1. To access the templates, log into your CreateSpace account and go to the following URL: https://www.createspace.com/en/community/docs

2. Select **Interior Templates** from the Popular Documents sidebar.

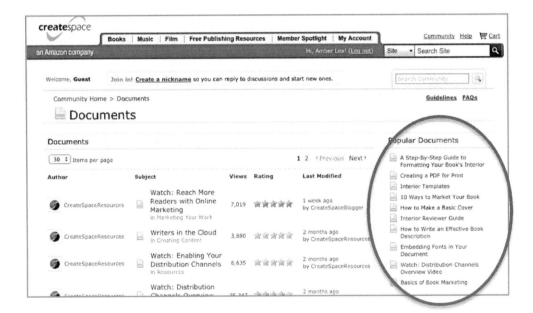

3. Once the "Interior Templates" window opens, scroll down to the **Basic Templates** column and download the book template that corresponds to the book size you've chosen.

Trim Size	**Formatted Templates** *These templates include sample content to guide you, including front matter, chapters, headers, page numbers, etc. Additional tips*	**Basic Templates** *These blank templates' page size and margins meet submission specifications. Just copy and paste your manuscript by section.*
5 x 8 inches	Download 5" x 8" Formatted Template	Download 5" x 8" Basic Template
5.06 x 7.81 inches	Download 5.06" x 7.81" Formatted Template	Download 5.06" x 7.81" Basic Template
5.25 x 8 inches	Download 5.25" x 8" Formatted Template	Download 5.25" x 8" Basic Template
5.5 x 8.5 inches	Download 5.5" x 8.5" Formatted Template	Download 5.5" x 8.5" Basic Template
6 x 9 inches	Download 6" x 9" Formatted Template	Download 6" x 9" Basic Template

4. After downloading your book template, open it with Microsoft Word.

5. Now, open up your chapbook, select all of the text (Cmd-A on the Mac, Ctrl-A on the PC) and copy and paste it into the template. Don't worry about what it looks like at this point — it'll be messy.

6. Close your original chapbook.

7. Save your newly pasted chapbook under its name followed by DRAFT and the date. Example: My Chapbook_DRAFT_01-19-14.

8. You now have a chapbook that'll look something like the following, if it's prose:

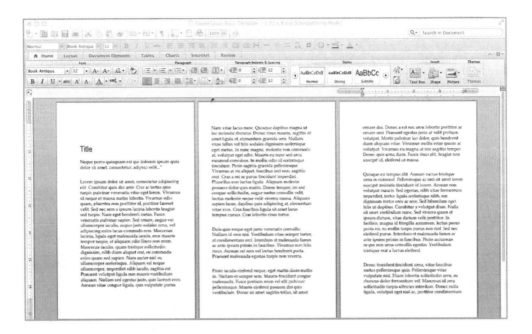

And something like this if it's poetry:

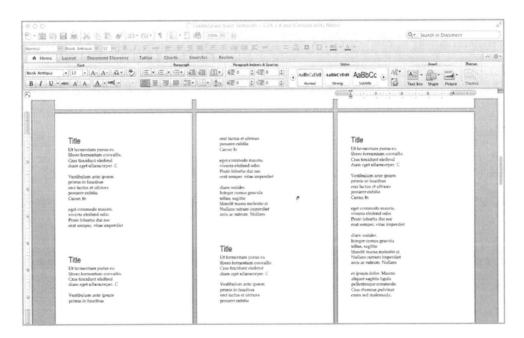

9. If you plan to include images in your chapbook, copy the images into a subfolder inside your chapbook document folder. During Week 3 we will cover the basics of how to insert images into your manuscript and how to format them.

Reflection

- What were the easiest and most difficult parts of this week's work. What made them seem easy or difficult?

- What was new to you?

- What was most valuable?

- What are your thoughts about this stage of the publishing process?

Week 3: Fixing Formatting Issues & Using Styles

What Are Styles?

When a writer has not yet learned how to use Word's styles, she applies all her formatting manually. For example, to format a title, she might select the title, apply bold formatting, make it a slightly larger font size, and center it.

Applying formatting in this manner is called "direct formatting." If you generally use direct formatting you'll know it can be a tedious process. For example, to format all the titles in your book, you would have to repeat the direct formatting process for each title, being careful to select the same paragraph formatting and font size every time. It's easy to make mistakes, unintentionally varying the formatting; after all that work, you might still end up with a manuscript that doesn't look as good as you want.

Also, manuscripts formatted by direct formatting are difficult to update. If you want to change the look of the document, you have to manually select each element (titles, prose paragraphs, etc.) and apply your new formatting.

By contrast, using styles to format your manuscript allows you to quickly and easily apply a set of formatting choices consistently throughout your manuscript.

So what is a style? According to Microsoft, "A style is a set of formatting characteristics, such as font name, size, color, paragraph alignment and spacing."

How do styles work? Using the title-formatting example above, instead of taking three separate steps to format your heading as 16-point, bold Cambria, you could achieve the same result in one step by applying Word's built-in Heading 1 style. For each title in your manuscript, you'd just click in the heading (you don't even need to select all the text), and then click Heading 1 in the gallery of styles.

This week, you're going to create and apply styles to all elements of your manuscript. But before you begin working with styles, you'll need to examine your manuscript for six direct formatting errors writers commonly make.

The Six Formatting Don'ts and Their Corresponding Do's

For your work to have a professional appearance, you will want to learn and adhere to a few rules. There are many more than the six that follow, but I consider these to be the most basic and important. Learning and using these guidelines on a consistent basis, even when drafting, will improve the overall look of your writing *and* make it easier to edit.

Your first task this week is to fix your formatting so that it conforms to the Do's described below. Follow the step-by-step instructions (shown after the guidelines) for how to accomplish numbers 1, 3, 4, 5, and 6. We will use Word Styles (explained later in this lesson) to accomplish number 2 and the last half of 5.

Six Important Guidelines:

1. **Don't** use paragraph returns to move text to the next page.
    Do use Page or Section breaks.

2. **Don't** use extra returns to format space between paragraphs.
    Do use "space before" and "space after" paragraph formatting options.

3. **Don't** use a return to create a line break in a paragraph of prose.
    Do use a return at the end of each paragraph.

4. **Don't** use spaces to format text on the page. Most fonts are not mono-width, which means each space is a different size and your formatting will not line up correctly when printed, even if it looks right on your computer screen.
    Do use paragraph formatting or tabs to format text on a page.

5. **Don't** use tabs or spaces to indent the first line of a paragraph.
    Do use First Line Indent in your paragraph formatting dialogue box.

6. **Don't** use two spaces between sentences.

    Do use one space between sentences.

Before beginning the following steps, open the draft of your chapbook (be sure you're viewing it in print layout mode) and save with a new name, such as: Chapbook Title_draftv2_Date.docx.

Then, turn on Show Nonprintable Characters. On both the Mac and the PC, this is accomplished by clicking the paragraph (🔳) icon in your Toolbar. Activating this feature will enable you to see all paragraph returns, spaces, pages breaks, tabs, and so on.

Complete all of the following steps. After each step, save your work.

Removing Extra Paragraph Returns Within Prose

You rarely need more than one extra paragraph return between paragraphs. Instead, space between titles and text, whether poetry or prose, should be handled using the paragraph formatting options in Word. To quickly remove any extra paragraph returns using Word's Find/Replace feature:

1. Move your cursor to the start of your document.

2. Activate Find and Replace. On the Mac, this is done by pressing Cmd-Shift-H. On the PC, press Ctrl-H or press Ctrl-F to activate the Find panel, then pull down the menu next to the Find box and select Replace.

Selecting Replace On the PC:

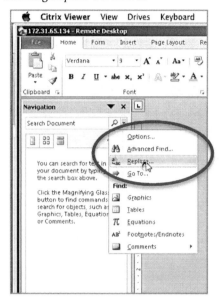

3. In the Find box enter "^p^p^p" (^p is Word's symbol for a paragraph return) without the quotation marks.

4. In the Replace box enter "^p^p". It will look like the following:

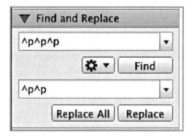

5. Click Replace All.

6. Repeat Number 5 (clicking Replace All) until Word can find no more matches for three paragraph returns in a row.

If, as many writers do, you used paragraph returns to move a title to a new page, you will find that removing extra paragraph returns moved the titles of each of your pieces to appear directly under the end of the previous piece. In the following example, you can see that the title, "Storm Clouds," now appears directly under the end of the previous poem. (You may see one paragraph return between the end of a piece and a title.)

Don't be concerned about the placement of your titles at this time. When we begin using Word's Style feature later in this chapter, we will take care of this placement issue.

> tears the color of mud puddles. ¶
> STORM CLOUDS ¶
> ¶

Removing Paragraph Returns Within A Paragraph Of Prose

Writers sometimes enter a paragraph return to force a line break in the middle of a paragraph. As you will understand when we apply styles, this is a big "no-no."
There are two types of paragraph returns, soft and hard. A hard return will appear as a "¶" at the end of a line, while a soft return will appear as a "↵" at the end of a line, like so:

> se, outlives the marriage, ↵
> to care. ¶

If you intentionally or unintentionally inserted returns *within* a paragraph, the fix must be done manually.

1. Starting at the beginning of your chapbook scroll through the entire book looking for paragraph returns (either hard or soft) at the end of lines in the middle of what is supposed to be one paragraph.

2. Delete the paragraph return and insert a space instead. (If there is already a space, do not insert a second one.)

Removing First Line Tabs

First line indents should always be made using Word's Paragraph Formatting specifications. In this step, we're going to remove all tabs at the beginning of paragraphs. If you want first line indents, you'll handle that part of the formatting when you learn how to use styles. For now:

1. Activate Word's Find/Replace feature (Cmd-Shift-H on the Mac or Ctrl-H on the PC).

2. In the Find box enter "^p^t" (the symbol for a paragraph return followed by a tab) and in the Replace box enter "^p" (a paragraph return).

3. Click the Replace All button.

4. Continue to click the Replace All button until Word finds no more matches.

Removing Spaces Used for Formatting

Using spaces to indent lines of text or poetry is another common mistake. Unfortunately, this mistake results in a printed work with uneven left margins or, at the very least, does not achieve the intended results.

You can use Word's Find/Replace function to remove these spaces, but I recommend you perform this fix visually and manually. The following steps lay the groundwork for creating and applying a poetry Style.

1. Starting at the beginning of your chapbook scroll through the entire book looking for spaces used for formatting. Here are a couple of common examples:

   Example A — Indenting second lines of poetry

   > I·slid·inside·the·foreign·world·of·you ¶
   > ·····Needing·your·touch ¶
   > ·····The·welcome·of·your·smile ¶

Example B — Formatting Titles

2. Delete all spaces at the beginning of a line. In Example B above, the title will now align to the left margin.

    If the spaces were used to indent the first line of a paragraph, the paragraph will now align to the left margin. Leave it this way for now.

    If the spaces are used for poetry as in Example A above, continue to step number 3.

3. Replace the paragraph return for the lines that belong together with a soft return, as in the following example. To insert a soft return, highlight the hard return and replace it by pressing Shift-Return. End each stanza with a hard return.

    Example of stanza with soft returns at the end of all lines except the last.

    I slid inside the foreign world of you ↵
    Needing your touch ↵
    The welcome of your smile ¶

Now that you've done the groundwork, you'll easily achieve the hanging indent effect you wanted by creating and applying a poetry style (directions for creating and applying a poetry style are given later in this chapter). And, most importantly, the indented lines will align perfectly and professionally.

Removing Extra Spaces Between Sentences

Many of us learned to enter two spaces between sentences, but today's publishing standards require one space between sentences.

It can be difficult to retrain oneself to enter only one space after each sentence. Fortunately, if you still have a tendency to press that spacebar twice (a quick look at your manuscript will reveal the truth), here's a simple fix.

1. Activate Word's Find/Replace feature (Cmd-Shift-H on the Mac or Ctrl-H on the PC).

2. In the Find box enter two spaces. You won't be able to see them, but trust your fingers.

3. In the Replace box enter one space.

4. Click the Replace All button. Continue to click the Replace All button until Word finds no more matches.

Using Styles

As discussed at the beginning of this chapter, "Styles" is a powerful feature that allows you to quickly format an entire document and generate an automated table of contents. Once you learn to use Styles, you'll never look back!

Choosing Your Fonts — The Look And Feel Of Your Book

Professional publications rarely use more than two fonts: one used for titles and one for the text. Typically, a serif font is used for the text and a sanserif font is used for the title, but this can be reversed with a serif font for the title and a sans serif for the text. A serif is a small decorative line added as embellishment to the basic form of a letter. The font used for this text is a serif font. A common sans serif typeface is Helvetica.

Examples of serif fonts include Adobe Garamond, Cambria, and Century Schoolbook.

Examples of sanserif fonts include Calibri, Arial, and ayutha.

I suggest experimenting with fonts until you find two that you like and that work well together.

Once you've selected the font(s) for your chapbook, you can begin creating the styles you'll use for your chapter titles, stanzas of poetry, and prose.

Create and Apply a Chapter Title Style

The easiest way to create and apply a style is to direct format a title or paragraph of text and then create a style based on the formatted text. The following steps walk you through this simple process.

1. Select the title of your first piece. Be sure to select the whole line, including the paragraph return at the end.

2. Apply your title font. (In the illustration shown after step 5, I used a 13 pt. Gill Sans Light font.)

3. Next, open the Paragraph Formatting dialog box.

    On the Mac

    • Select Paragraph from the Format menu (or press Command-Option-M).

    On the PC

    • Click the Formatting button on the toolbar as shown here:

4. Click the Line and Page Breaks tab and select Page break before. After you create and apply your Chapter Title style, each title will automatically be placed on a new page.

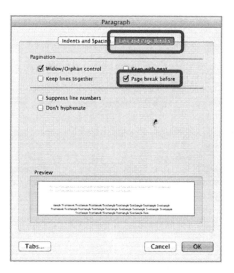

5. Click the Indents and Spacing tab and specify the alignment, space before, and space after your title. In the example shown below, I have specified centered alignment, no left or right indentation, 36 pt. before my title (which pushes it further down the page, and 13 pt after, which gives some space between the title and the text that follows it.

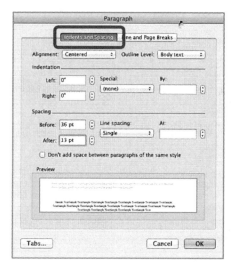

The formatted title.

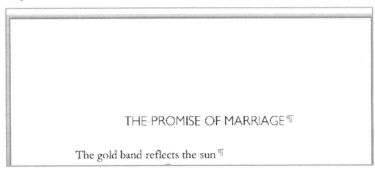

Now that you have the "model" title, use it to create the "Chapter Title" style:

6. Place your cursor anywhere in the title.

On the Mac

*   Pull down the Format Menu and select Style. Click the New Button, give your style a name (I've used Chapter Title in the example), click OK, and then click Apply.

On the PC

- Right-click the title, select Styles, and Save Selection as New Quick Style. Enter a name (Chapter Title) and click OK.

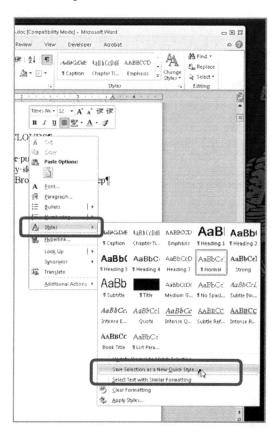

The final step is to apply the style to every title in the Manuscript.

7. Scroll down to your next title. Click anywhere within the title, and then click on Chapter Title in the Styles menu. That's all it takes!

On a Mac:

- Select the style from the drop-down menu on the toolbar in one of two places: the quick style menu on the Home tab or the drop-down menu in the formatting ribbon.

The quick style menu on a Mac

The drop-down style menu

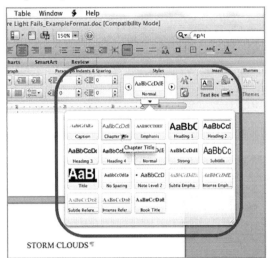

On a PC:

- Select the style from the Quick Styles menu on the Home tab.

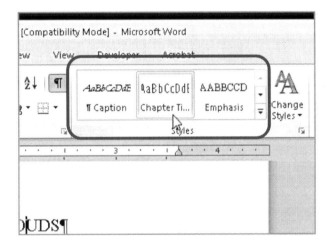

Now, when you decide to change something about your titles — for example, you want them further down on the page, or you decide you'd like them to be a different font or font size — all you have to do is modify the title style and, *voilà!,* all your titles are instantly and magically changed at once, without the tedious process of highlighting and direct formatting each one.

Modifying Styles

To make a change to a style:

1. right click on the style in the Quick Styles menu and select Modify...

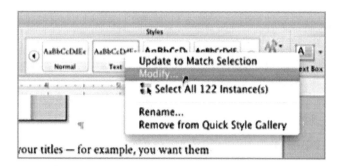

2. Select the type of formatting you want to change from the drop-down Format menu, such as paragraph formatting to change line spacing or font formatting to change font type or size.

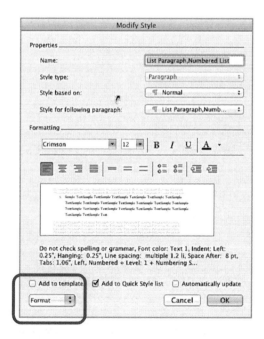

3. Specify your changes in the dialogue boxes and click OK. All the text to which that style was applied will now conform to the changes you made.

At this point, I encourage you to play a little with modifying styles just to see how wonderfully it works. For the sake of experimentation, go ahead and modify your Chapter Title style so that your titles are 36 pts. and bold. Scroll through your document to see what happened. Now change the style back to the way you like it.

It really is magic, isn't it!

Create and Apply Your Subheading Style(s)

The process for creating and applying styles to the subheadings and the body of your work, whether poetry or prose, is exactly the same as for titles.

If your manuscript has subheadings, repeat the above directions to create and apply a subheading style — substituting the desired font size, alignment, and line spacing — and then apply to all the subheadings in your manuscript. You may choose to use either the same font as your Chapter Title style or the font you selected for Prose. Play around with it and see what works for you.

Create and Apply Your Prose Paragraph Style

1. Direct format a paragraph of prose the way you like it, create a new style using the directions above, and then apply to all the prose in your manuscript.

    For prose, I suggest using an 11 point font (12 pt. may appear too large in a 5.5 x 8.5 inch book). Set the paragraph formatting to justified with a first line indent of about .3" and a multiple line spacing of 1.2 or 1.3 lines. (See illustration below.)

> ◼ ¶
>
> ### IN CASE MOTHER WAS WRONG ¶
>
> The bed of brown leaves you lay me on smells of ancient fires and broken promises. Each twist and contortion causes them to crunch beneath my skin scolding me as I open myself to the demon in you. From the corner of my eye I spy a rotten apple with rust colored bruises like the scarlet letter sewn invisibly over my heart. When I rise the maple and mimosa leaves imprint my thighs like fossils. ¶
>
> Days later, when we are over, I hide indoors. Bare branches scrape the windows pointing fingers. The howl of autumn wind is a sorrowful priest. I imagine that if I open my front door and step into the apple crisp air everyone will see what I have become. There are no leaves on the trees to tuck secrets behind in late October. ¶

Create and Apply Your Poetry Style(s)

If you have poetry in more than one format, for example some that is left-aligned and some that is centered, you'll want to create a style for each format. In this case, repeat the style creation process and apply to each stanza of your poems.

Remember, way back in the first part of this chapter, when you replaced hard returns for soft returns at the end of every line of poetry except for the last line of the stanza? Perhaps you also removed spaces you used to indent some of the lines.

The following steps show you how to create a style that will give you the result shown in the following illustration. Notice the soft return before the indented lines, and the lack of spaces used at the beginning of those same lines.

> ‖
> I slid inside the foreign world of you ↵
> Needing your touch ↵
> The welcome of your smile ¶

This is called a hanging indent. To create a hanging indent for your poetry style:

1. Highlight a stanza of poetry.

2. Open your paragraph dialogue box.

3. Specify a first line hanging indent of .3" (or whatever value between .25" and .5" you prefer to use). You may also set your line spacing to a multiple of 1.3, to 1.5 or double, or whatever works for the look of your book.

   When you have finished with the format specifications, click OK. Your stanza should now look like the above example.

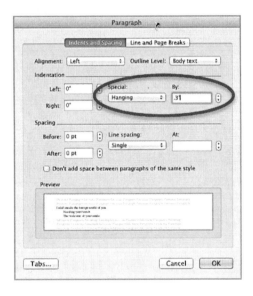

Here are a few formatting suggestions when creating styles for poetry:

- As instructed above, use a soft return at the end of each line except for the last line dividing stanzas (see illustration below).

- Indent the left line until the poetry looks good on the page, and use this same indent (.25" perhaps) for every left-aligned poem. This will give consistency to the overall look of your chapbook, and give your poetry more space on the page.

- Set the paragraph formatting Space After to somewhere between 8 and 12 pts. and remove the extra paragraph return between stanzas.

- In the example below, I used 11 pt. Garamond with multiple of 1.3 for line spacing (same as the prose), with an 8 pt. space after paragraph specification.

> **YOU·ARE·PROBABLY·WELL·AWARE** ¶
>
> That·sin·can·live·in·the·hearts ↵
> of·the·best·of·us—— ↵
> invisible·dust·mites ↵
> with·barbed·legs. ¶
>
> Awkward·wrong·choices ↵
> cling·to·our·best·intentions, ↵
> despite·Kohlberg's·moral·theories. ¶

When the formatting for your "model" stanza looks the way you want it, use it to create a new "Poetry" style. Then, apply the style to all your poems. Remember, you can always make a change to the Poetry style, which will then automatically change every stanza to which the style was applied.

Reflection

Take a moment to write about this week's progress.

- What were the easiest and most difficult parts of this week's work. What made them seem easy or difficult?

- What did you learn?

- What are your thoughts about this stage of the publishing process?

Week 4: Completing the Interior

During Week 3, you fixed formatting issues and formatted and applied styles to all your prose and poetry. This week you will:

- Insert pictures or scanned artwork where desired
- Create and format front matter: title page and table of contents
- Format headers and pagination
- Proofread
- Save in PDF format and upload to CreateSpace

Inserting Pictures or Scanned Artwork

If you have not yet added pictures to your manuscript and you intend to do so, you'll want to add them now. If you don't want or need to add images, skip to the next section, Creating and Formatting Front Matter.

Before inserting images, you need to make sure they are of print quality and resolution. This means a resolution of at least 300 pixels per inch.

If you're using photos taken on a cell phone or digital camera, or artwork that has been scanned on a high-resolution scanner, the images should be fine. But it's always good practice to check and fix the resolution if necessary.

Checking Image Resolution

On a Mac:

- Open the image in Preview.
- Select Adjust Size from the Tools Menu and look at the photo size in the Image Dimensions dialog box.

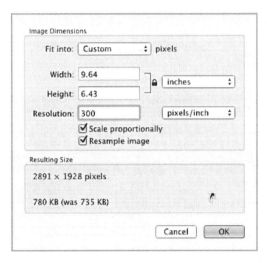

- If your desired print size is 3 inches by 3 inches, then the dimensions should be at least 900 x 900 pixels. In the above example, 9.64 by 6.43 inches = 2891 x 1928 pixels (9.64 x 300 = 2891 and 6.43 x 300 = 1928).

- If the image is not a high enough resolution, you can resize it by changing the width and height dimensions and then clicking OK.

Caution: Always work on a copy of your image, not the original. And don't enlarge an image more than 10%, as the result may be too pixelated or blurry to be of professional print quality.

On a PC:

- Open the image in Windows Photo Viewer or another image editor.

- In Windows Photo Viewer, select Properties from the File Menu and scroll down to view the Image Dimensions, as shown on the following page.

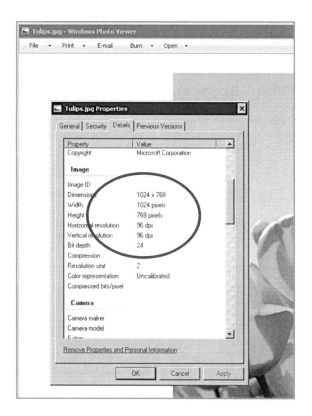

In this example, the picture is 1024 x 768. 1024 ÷ 300 = 3.4 and 768 ÷ 300 = 2.56. So the maximum printable size for this image is 3.4 x 2.56 inches.

Inserting, Placing, and Formatting Images in Word

Once you know your images are the correct size, you can insert them into your manuscript. Please note that a complete tutorial on how to manage images in Word is beyond the scope of this book. The following steps will lead you through the simple process of inserting an image from your computer into your manuscript.

1. Place your cursor where you want to locate the image.

2. Drag and drop a photo from a folder on your computer to the document, or:

   On a Mac:
   - Select Photo from the Insert menu and then select Picture From File. Locate the picture in your Finder window and double click to insert it into your document.

- Once the picture is inserted, you can resize it by dragging the corner selection guides. Hold down the Shift key while resizing to maintain the image aspect ratio.

On a PC:

- Click the Insert Tab on the Ribbon.

- Click the Picture Icon

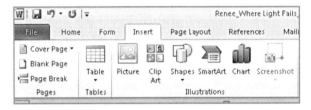

- Locate the picture on your hard drive and double click to insert it into your document. Hold down the Shift key while resizing to maintain the image aspect ratio.

3. Once the image is placed, you can format its alignment just as you would text — left-aligned, centered, or right-aligned. There are many other adjustments you can make, such as line spacing and indenting. Experiment to find the right look for your manuscript.

From Color to Black and White

If your image is in color, and your chapbook's interior is to be printed in black and white you can use Word's formatting features to adjust color saturation and contrast.

On both PC and Mac:

1. Double-click the image to activate the Format Picture tab on the ribbon.

2. Select 0% saturation from the Recolor drop-down menu as shown.

3. If you want to adjust the contrast or sharpen the image, use the Corrections drop-down menu. Experiment to find the look you want.

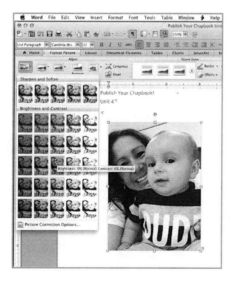

Creating and Formatting Front Matter

Your chapbook front matter will include, at minimum, a title page, copyright page, and table of contents. You may also choose to include pages for dedication and acknowledgements. (Acknowledgements can be placed at the end of the chapbook, just before the author bio, if you prefer.)

Title Page

1. To add a title page, place your cursor at the beginning of your manuscript and insert a page break.

    You'll then have a blank page with a Page Break at the top as seen below.

2. Place your cursor *before* the Page Break symbol, and then fill in and format your title page. I've given the following as an example; however, you will want to choose fonts and formatting that complement your book. It may also be helpful to browse title pages of books in your library for ideas.

    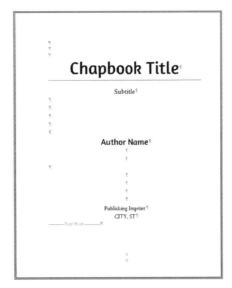

Copyright Page

To add a copyright page, repeat the step of placing your cursor at the beginning of your first Chapter (or piece) Title and inserting a page break.

Then place your cursor *before* the page break symbol and enter the following text, substituting appropriate title and author information and using returns to move it to the bottom of the page:

Copyright © YEAR by Author Name.

All rights reserved. No part of this publication may be reproduced, distributed or transmitted in any form or by any means, including photocopying, recording, or other electronic or mechanical methods, without the prior written permission of the publisher, except in the case of brief quotations embodied in critical reviews and certain other noncommercial uses permitted by copyright law. For permission requests, write to the publisher at the address below.

Author/Publishing Company Name

Street Address

City, State/Province Postal-Code

www.website-url.com

Book Title/ Author Name. —1st ed.

ISBN 10: 0000000000

ISBN 13: 978-0-0000000-0-0

The Result should look something like the following illustration. The format and placement of text on the copyright page is arbitrary. Usually, text on copyright pages is in a smaller font size than in the rest of the book (9 or 10 pt.) and formatted so that it hugs the bottom of the page. (Notice that in this case I used paragraph returns to move the text to the bottom of the page. Every rule has its exceptions and, for me, this is one of them.)

Copyright © 2013 by Author Name. ¶
¶
All rights reserved. No part of this publication may be reproduced, distributed or transmitted in any form or by any means, including photocopying, recording, or other electronic or mechanical methods, without the prior written permission of the publisher, except in the case of brief quotations embodied in critical reviews and certain other noncommercial uses permitted by copyright law. For permission requests, write to the publisher at the address below. ¶
¶
Author/Publishing Company Name ¶
Street Address ¶
City, State/Province Postal Code ¶
www.website-url.com ¶
¶
Book Title/ Author Name. —1st ed. ¶
ISBN 10: ¶
ISBN 13: 978-0-0000000-0-0 ¶
¶
————————Page Break———————— ¶

If you are using a CreateSpace assigned ISBN, then you need to get the correct numbers from your account on CreateSpace.

If you have purchased your own ISBN number from Bowker, enter the appropriate numbers on the copyright page.

Creating a Table of Contents

It is at this point in the formatting process that you will truly begin to understand the power of Styles, if you haven't already. To add a Table of Contents (TOC) page, place your cursor at the beginning of the title to your first piece and insert an Odd Page Section Break. An Odd Page Section Break ensures that the next page will begin on an odd page.

On a Mac:

- Pull down the Insert menu and select Break/Section Break (odd page).

On a PC:

- Select the Page Layout tab on the Ribbon and select Odd Page from the Breaks pull down menu.

You'll have a blank page with the section break at the top of it.

Adding a TOC on the Mac

1. Place your cursor *before* the section break, Type "Contents," and press return to give yourself an extra line of space.

2. Select Index and Tables… from the Insert Menu.

3. In the resulting Dialog box, select the Table of Contents Tab. I suggest using the "From template" format because it will pull the font styles from your template. Adjust the number of levels you want to show — for most, it will be only one level, the Chapter Title.

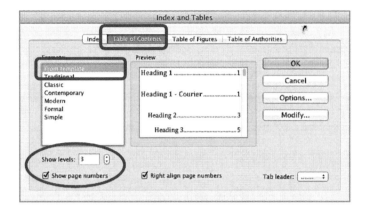

4. Click the Options button to specify which styles to include in the TOC. Scroll down the list of available styles. In most cases, you'll see Heading 1, 2, and 3 (or however many levels you specified) automatically selected.

   In order to remove unwanted Heading styles from inclusion, delete the numbers from the TOC level fields so they are blank.

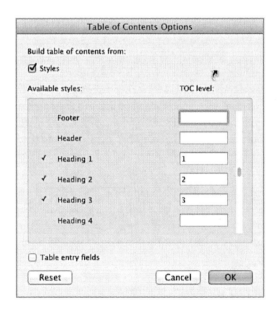

5. Scroll down (or up) the list of Available Styles until you see your Chapter Title style. Enter a "1" in the TOC level field.

If you have a subhead style that you want to include in the TOC, enter a "2" in that style's TOC level field.

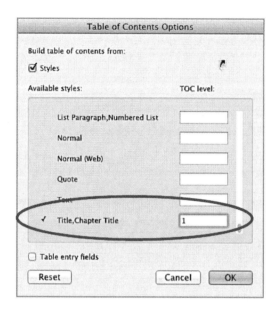

6. Click OK, and your Table of Contents will automatically populate on your Table of Contents page.

7. You can format the table of contents any way you wish at this point, and you may need to make some adjustments.

    Just be careful because the entire TOC is a field and it's easy to select the delete the entire table by mistake. If that happens, press Command-Z to Undo.

8. Finally, apply your Chapter Title style to the "Contents" heading.

Adding a TOC on the PC

1. Select the References tab on the ribbon, then select a Insert Table of Contents from the Table of Contents pull down menu.

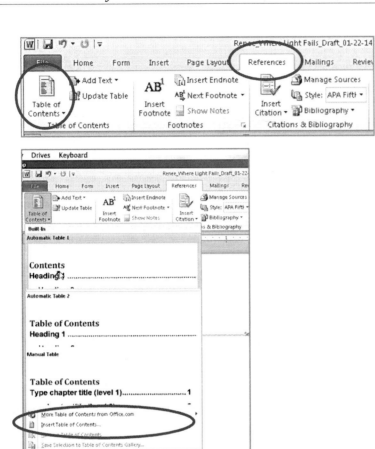

2. Follow steps 2-8 for the Mac

Adding and Formatting Headers

Follow these steps to add headers to your book:

1. On the first page of your first piece, double-click in the header section (above the text in the margin). If the ribbon doesn't automatically switch to the Header and Footer tab, click the tab to reveal the formatting options.

   On a Mac:

   On a PC:

   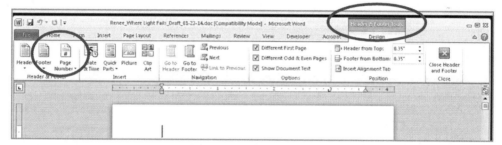

2. Check the "Different Odd & Even Pages" option. Now, because this page falls after the Odd Page Section Break at the end of the table of contents, whatever you enter in this header will be repeated on every odd page.

3. If it's already checked, uncheck the "Different First Page" option.

4. Deselect "Link to Previous" checkbox. This unlinks the header and footer of this section from the header and footer of the previous section, which, at this point, includes your title and copyright pages and table of contents.

5. In the header, enter the title of your chapbook.

6. Enter the page number by clicking on the Page Number icon in the Header and Footer ribbon, as shown above.

As you can see from the example here, I entered the chapbook title and page number, right justified and in my choice of header font.

You may choose to italicize your header or have it be all caps. The design choice is yours. (You may choose to leave the number close to the title or use spaces or a tab to separate them.)

Notice that in the illustration it shows as "page 3," even though it's the first piece in the document. Next, let's fix the numbering so that Page 1 starts *after* the table of contents.

With your cursor still in the header of the first piece:

On a Mac:

• Pull down the Insert menu and select Page Numbers ....

• Then click the Format button and in the resulting dialog box, click on "Start at:" and enter "1."

• Click OK.

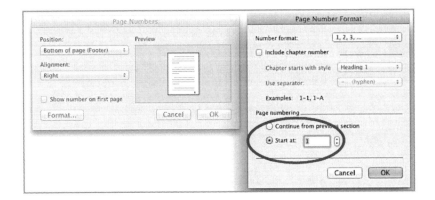

On a PC:

- Select Format Page Numbers from the Page Numbers drop-down menu on the Header and Footer Tools tab.

- You should now see a "1" in the header of the first title of your chapbook.

7. Place your cursor in the header of the next page. This will be your even page header. Left justify the page number and your name, as in the following example. The choice of font and style should match that in the odd page header.

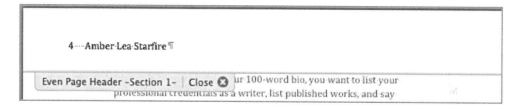

8. Scroll up to view your book title, copyright, and TOC pages. If your headers are showing up on these pages, double-click in the header section on any of these pages and delete the text in the header. Because the headers in the front matter section are not linked to the following section, deleting the text here will not affect the following pages.

9. Close the header by clicking close. (On the PC, the Close Header and Footer button is on the ribbon.) And save your work.

Updating the Table of Contents

Because the TOC calculated page numbers before we added headers and fixed the pagination, you'll need to update the TOC.

1. Right-click anywhere within the table of contents and select Update Field.

2. Select Update Page Numbers Only from the resulting dialogue box and click OK.

Magic!

Anytime you make a change that affects pagination, you can update your table of contents automatically, by simply right-clicking and updating page numbers again.

Adding a Dedication Page

A dedication page is typically placed after the table of contents and before your first piece. To add it, place your cursor just *before* the Section Break at the bottom of the table of contents page and add another Odd Section Break.

This will create another right-hand page. Add and format your dedication. Because this page also ends with an Odd Page Section Break, your first piece will remain on a right-side page, as page 1.

Proofreading Your Manuscript

At this point, you have a beautifully formatted chapbook, with headers, page numbering and a Table of Contents.

The next step is to print out and proofread your entire manuscript. *Do not skip this step!* And do not try to proofread on your computer screen! Print it out, take it away from your writing area, sit in a comfortable chair, and read it carefully. Look for every stray space, every double period. In short, anything that is incorrect or out of place.

Ask a writing friend with editing skills to help.

Saving Your Manuscript as a PDF

Finally, you're ready to save your manuscript interior as a PDF and upload to CreateSpace!

On a Mac:
When saving a Word document in PDF format on a Mac, the computer uses the default printer page size, so that even if your document size is specified as 6 by 9-inches, the PDF document will be created on 8.5 by 11-inch, letter-sized paper (assuming that's your default). To get around this:

1. Open System Preferences.

2. Select the Print and Scan button.

3. Pull down the default paper size menu and select your book's paper size. (In this example, it's 8 by 10 inches.)

4. Close the Preferences Window

5. In Word, select Save As from the File Menu and save as type PDF.

6. Open the PDF using Adobe Reader to ensure that everything looks the way you want it. When you're satisfied with your manuscript's appearance, change the default paper size back to letter.

On a PC:

1. Select select Save As from the File Menu, and save as type PDF.

2. Open the PDF using Adobe Reader to ensure that everything looks the way you want it to.

When you want to make corrections or adjustments, make the changes in your original Word manuscript and re-save as a PDF.

Uploading Your Chapbook Interior to CreateSpace

One of the great things about CreateSpace is that once your PDF interior is uploaded, CreateSpace runs an automated print check of the document to ensure there are no problems that will affect the quality of your finished book.

If there are problems, you can correct them, re-save your document as a PDF and re-upload without any extra charges.

To upload your book interior:

1. Log into CreateSpace and click on the title of your chapbook. If you haven't yet done so, complete the Title Information and ISBN sections. Then,

2. Click the Interior hyperlink on the Setup tab.

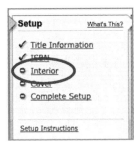

3. Select Upload Your Book File and click the Browse button to select the PDF file you created and saved on your computer.

4. Scroll to the bottom of the page and click Save to upload the book.

5. CreateSpace will run the print check, inform you when it is completed, and alert you to any problems.

Reflection

You've just completed two week's worth of intense formatting. Take a moment to celebrate and reflect by journaling about your process before continuing.

- Did you learn many new skills this week, or was much of this "old hat" for you?

- What was most challenging for you, and how did you deal with that challenge?

- How do you feel now that your interior has been uploaded to CreateSpace?

- What will you do to celebrate your accomplishment?

Week 5: Creating Your Cover & Completing Setup

Cover Creator

The next step is to create a cover for your book. There are several ways to accomplish this:

- Create a cover using software such as Photoshop, Adobe Illustrator, or InDesign and upload to CreateSpace.

- Hire a designer to create a cover.

- Hire CreateSpace to design a cover for you.

- Use CreateSpace's online Cover Creator, which offers an array of pre-formatted templates, artwork, and fonts for users to create a cover on the fly.

If this book were about publishing a book-length work, I would recommend hiring a designer to create your cover. However, for the purposes of creating a chapbook, I think you'll find CreateSpace's Cover Creator offers enough different templates and flexibility for a satisfying cover.

Before beginning, watch CreateSpace's official video about how to use Cover Creator. The video provides an overview of the interface and Cover Creator's capabilities.

Log into CreateSpace, enter the following URL into your browser:
https://createspacecommunity.s3.amazonaws.com/Video%20Tutorials/CCVT%20Final_1.mp4

Now that you have a sense of what Cover Creator can do, let's get started.

1. From your Member Dashboard, click the link to your chapbook.

2. Select the Cover link from the Setup tab.

3. Select a finish for your book cover: matte or glossy.

4. Under "Choose how to submit the cover of your book:" select Build Your Cover Online, and click the Launch Cover Creator button.

5. A window will open with the first set of design templates.

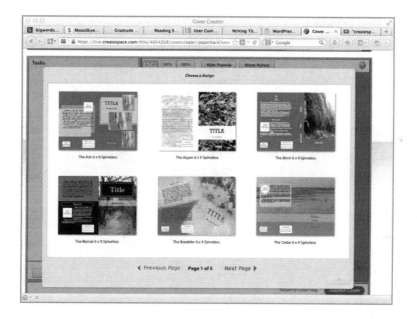

6. Page through the designs until you find a basic layout that you like. Double-click a design to select it.

7. Remember that you are not limited by the colors or images currently displayed on any of the templates. And you can change a template at any time during the process.

8. Each template offers several "themes." Pull down the theme menu to change the font used on the cover in order to find one that is the closest match to the tone your want your cover to have.

Once you've selected your theme, click the next button. If you don't like any of the fonts offered with that template, you may choose a different template by clicking the Change Design button at the bottom of the window, below the template menu.

9. Under the Title drop-down section of the menu, you can change how the title will be displayed on your book.

10. Some templates also offer the option to display a subtitle. If you want the subtitle to display, make sure the Visible checkbox is selected, enter your subtitle, and click the Apply button.

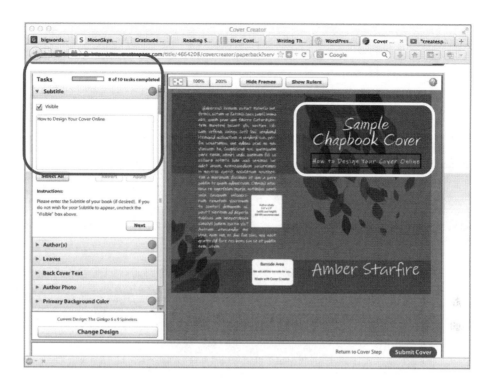

11. Each template is different. In the example above, the next two items on the menu are Author(s) and Leaves. Author(s) allows you to change how your name will be displayed on the cover. The Leaves menu item allows you to choose whether or not the graphic leaf elements are visible.

12. In the next example, I've changed the design for my Sample Chapbook. Notice how the menu items on the left have also changed, containing more options such as:

- Front Cover Image

- Old Paper

- About the Author

- Background color (instead of Primary Background Color), and

- Font Color

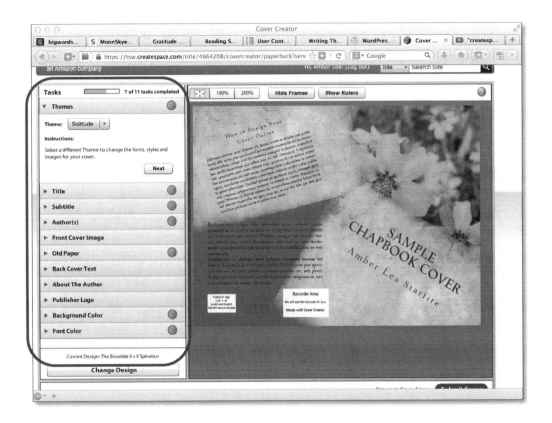

Changing options, such as color and background image can drastically affect the overall look of the cover:

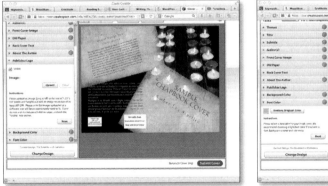 

Now it's your turn. Play around with the different templates, colors, and available images (you can upload your own image as well), until you have a cover that suits your needs.

13. Finally, click the Submit Cover button.

14. CreateSpace will create a full online preview. Carefully review the design and content of the cover. If needed, make changes and resubmit.

Completing the Setup

Once your cover is submitted, click the Complete Setup link on the Setup tab. You'll see the following screen (your details will be different, of course).

Carefully review all the information on the Complete Setup page, including:

- Title, subtitle (if any), and author name.

- The ISBN and publisher name, if you purchased an ISBN. If you opted for the free CreateSpace ISBN, CreateSpace will appear as the publisher.

- Type of paper and interior file name. (In the example above, I have not yet uploaded the interior. Yours should show the interior file as complete, along with the name of the uploaded PDF file.)

- Cover finish and cover as "cover-creator.pdf" (unless you uploaded a finished cover).

You can edit any of these items if necessary.

If everything looks good, submit your chapbook for review. CreateSpace will review the interior file, cover, and title information, and send you an email within 24 hours to let you know if there are any issues with the formatting.

Reflection

- Did you enjoy learning about and using CreateSpace's Cover Creator? Why or why not?

- What was most interesting or rewarding?

- What was least interesting or rewarding?

- How do you feel now that your book is nearly complete?

Week 6: The Final Steps

This week, you'll accomplish the final steps to publishing your chapbook, including selecting distribution channels, setting pricing, completing the book description and author bio information, ordering a proof copy — and publishing!

Selecting Your Chapbook's Distribution Channels

CreateSpace offers a number of distribution options depending upon the intended audience for your book. And each distribution channel has its own royalty structure.

- If you intend to make your chapbook available to friends and family but not to make your book available to the public, select only the CreateSpace eStore distribution channel. This will enable you to send the eStore link for your book to your mailing list or put it on your website. You will receive the highest royalties from books sold on the eStore. CreateSpace also allows you to set up promotional discount codes for eStore buyers — something you can't do on Amazon.

- If you plan to make your chapbook available for public sale, at the very least you'll want to select the three Standard Distribution channels for your chapbook: Amazon.com, which makes your chapbook available for sale on the Amazon.com website; Amazon Europe, which, as the name indicates, makes your chapbook available for sale on Amazon's European websites; and the CreateSpace eStore, already discussed.

To better understand distribution channels, watch this video on YouTube: http://www.youtube.com/watch?v=sN7QmaBcl08

For additional instructions about how to enable the different distribution channels and set pricing for your chapbook (I'll also cover pricing this week), watch this video: http://www.youtube.com/watch?v=iaS3ja6bLHw. Please note that though the video mentions a $25 fee, CreateSpace no longer charges for expanded distribution.

Setting Price

To set the price of your chapbook, select the Pricing link from the Distribution tab to open the Pricing window.

In the example for *Week by Week* below, you'll see that I've set the list price at $10.95 in U.S. dollars. Beneath the USD price field, CreateSpace displays the minimum list price for the book. You may not set the price below the minimum amount.

When you enter a list price into the field, CreateSpace calculates the royalty for each channel. In my example, when *Week by Week* is sold at the retail price of $10.95 on Amazon, I earn a royalty of $3.42. When it's sold from the CreateSpace eStore, it's $5.61. As you can see, it's to my advantage to sell the book from CreateSpace.

Because I have also selected Amazon Europe and Expanded distribution channels, CreateSpace automatically fills in the suggested retail amounts for British pounds and Euros and displays the royalties for each of those channels.

When setting the price for your chapbook, do a little research into similar publications and think about what you would pay for a chapbook like yours.

Cover Finish

You set the finish for your cover when you created the cover during Week 5; you can edit your choice by selecting the Cover Finish link in the Distribution tab.

Entering Book Description and Author Bio

Enter the description of your book into the Book Description field. This is the description that will be seen on the CreateSpace eStore and on Amazon. You may use the same description you added to the back of your book, or you may choose to expand this description for marketing and web display.

The same is true of the author bio field, which will also be displayed on Amazon and CreateSpace websites.

Selecting the BISAC Category

The Book Industry Standards and Communications (BISAC) category is important to help people find your chapbook, as well as the primary way it is listed on Amazon. To select a BISAC category, click the Choose… button to the right of the BISAC field. A window will open which allows you to select from a number of options. Scroll through the different categories and subcategories until you find one that is the closest category for your book. As the categories are limited, you may not always find one that is "exactly right," so select the categories that best fit your chapbook's content.

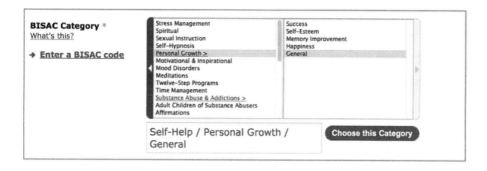

Keywords

Next, enter up to five keywords, separated by commas, for your work.

Here is what the completed Description page looks like:

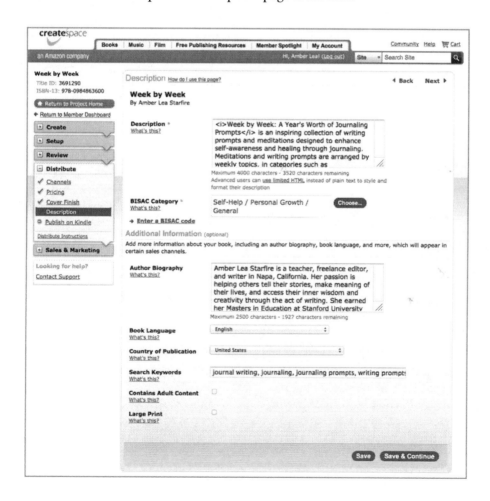

When you have completed the Description page information, click the Save button at the bottom of the page.

Clicking the Save & Continue button takes you to the Publish on Kindle page. CreateSpace does offer to convert your PDF files to Kindle for you at no cost. In general, because converting to Kindle from PDF tends to produce unreliable results, I recommend converting your book to Kindle and then uploading to the Kindle store. However, if you choose to try CreateSpace's conversion services, you will have an opportunity to review the results, and the book will not be published to Amazon Kindle without your consent.

Ordering a Proof

Finally, you've reached the next-to-final step in the publishing process — ordering a proof copy. While you may view your proof online, I *highly* recommend ordering a print copy to check the quality of your cover, interior images, font size, and so on.

To order a proof, click the Proof Your Book link under the Review tab on your Project Homepage. The link will become available after the book has passed CreateSpace's file review process, which will have a green checkmark next to it.

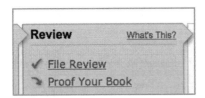

You pay only the cost of printing your book plus postage.

Don't Rush to Publication

When you receive your proof copy, review it thoroughly, including:

- Cover graphics and type (you might be surprised by how many typos get published on cover copy because self-publishers skipped this step), including placement and quality.

- Interior — carefully proofread every page. In addition to possible typos, note placement of text on the page, placement of headers and footers and page numbers, fonts, font size, and general appearance.

If needed, make changes to the interior and/or cover and re-upload your PDF file(s). If you make changes, order another proof copy and proofread again. Repeat this process until you are completely satisfied with the appearance and content of your book.

Publish!

Finally, the day you have been waiting for has arrived — the day you publish your chapbook! Log into your CreateSpace account, go to the Proof Your Book link, and click the button indicating that you've proofed the book and are ready to publish.

If you selected Amazon's distribution channel(s), your book will be up on Amazon within a few days — sometimes in only hours.

I recommend buying a *minimum* of ten copies, to give away to friends and reviewers. Send everyone you know the link to the CreateSpace eStore page, and if you have a blog be sure to post an article about your chapbook along with a link to the eStore.

Final Reflection

You did it! Write your final thoughts and reflections about what you've gained through this publishing process.

One Last Step

Once you've published your chapbook, please email the eStore link to me: amber@writingthroughlife.com.

Now go out and celebrate!

Publishing Resources

Print On Demand Publishing

- Createspace.com (of course).

- IngramSpark.com: a popular print-on-demand (POD) printer and book distributor that is owned by Ingram.

- *A Self-Publisher's Companion: Expert Advice for Authors Who Want to Publish* (Joel Friedlander). Joel also has a great website, TheBookDesigner.com, with a wealth of information about both POD and e-book publishing.

- Independent Book Publishers Association (http://www.ibpa-online.org/): a little pricey, but if you get serious about publishing, worth joining.

E-book Conversion and Publishing

- KDP Tools and Resources - Amazon Kindle Direct Publishing: (*https://kdp.amazon.com/help?topicId=A3IWA2TQYMZ5J6*).

- Smashwords.com.

- http://www.pdf4kindle.com/: a free online PDF-to-Kindle converter. I haven't tested this yet, but it looks promising.

- Jutoh (www.jutoh.com/): an inexpensive app that is easy to use and helps you convert to every e-book format. I use this and highly recommend it.

- Scrivener (latteandliterature.com): a powerful authoring software that automates and simplifies e-book conversion. When converting to e-book, it doesn't handle images as well as I'd like but is well worth buying and learning how to use.

Acknowledgements

Even small books like this one result from the efforts of more than one person.

I would like to acknowledge and thank all my creative writing students for inspiring me to help them publish their small collections, and especially: Renee Cassese, who graciously gave me permission to use portions of her chapbook as illustrations; Lauren Ross, for her keen editor's eye; and Ann Lonstein for probing questions that helped me to troubleshoot and clarify instructions.

About the Author

Other Books by Amber Lea Starfire (available in paperback and e-book):

- *Not the Mother I Remember: A Memoir*

- *Week by Week: A Year's Worth of Journaling Prompts & Meditations*

Amber Lea Starfire is an author, editor, and creative writing teacher who feels fortunate to live with her sweetheart in beautiful Napa Valley, California. Co-editor of *Times They Were A-Changing: Women Remember the '60s & '70s* and Coordinator for the Story Circle Network's Online Classes Program, Amber loves empowering writers to write and share their stories.

Her work has appeared in literary journals and anthologies, including *Beyond Boundaries* and *Vintage Voices 2012: Call of the Wild*. Amber holds an MFA in Creative Writing from the University of San Francisco and an MA in Education from Stanford University. She is a member of the California Writers Club, Story Circle Network, National Association of Memoir Writers (NAMW), and International Association for Journal Writing (IAJW).

For more information, visit Amber's website: www.writingthroughlife.com.

Made in the USA
San Bernardino, CA
11 April 2016